Rain is water

Photography by John Pettitt

Rain comes down.

It comes out of the clouds.

Rain comes down on the house.

It runs down the windows.

Rain comes down on the roof.
The roof gets wet.

Rain comes down on the grass.

The grass gets wet.

Rain comes down on the trees.

The trees get wet.

Rain comes down

on the flowers in the garden.

The flowers in the garden get wet.

The dog gets wet
in the rain.

We get wet in the rain.

Rain is water.